Library of Congress Cataloging-in-Publication Data

Ganeri, Anita, 1961-
    Athletes and actors / Anita Ganeri
        p. cm. – (All in a day's work)
    Originally published: Great Britain : David West children's books, 1997.
    Includes index.
    ISBN 0-87226-664-8
    1. Greece–Social life and customs–Juvenile literature. 2.
Occupations–Greece–Juvenile literature. [1. Greece-Social life and customs.] I. Title.
II. Series.

DF78 .G26 2001
331.7'02'0938--dc21

First published in the United States in 2001 by
Peter Bedrick Books
A division of NTC/Contemporary Publishing Group, Inc.
4255 West Touhy Avenue, Lincolnwood (Chicago),
Illinois 60712 - 1975 U.S.A.
Copyright © 1997 David West Children's Books
Text copyright © 1997 Anita Ganeri

Consultant: Robert Morkot
Illustrators: Manuela Cappon (Virgil Pomfret Agency),
Francis Phillips, Ken Stott (B.L. Kearley Ltd)

Designed and produced in Great Britain by
David West 👫 Children's Books,
7 Princeton Court, 55 Felsham Road, London SW15 1AZ

First published in Great Britain in 1997 by
Heinemann Children's Reference, an imprint of
Heinemann Educational Publishers, Halley Court,
Jordan Hill, Oxford OX2 8EJ, a division of Reed
Educational and Professional Publishing Limited.

Printed in Italy.
International Standard Book Number: 0-87226-664-8
10 9 8 7 6 5 4 3 2 1

ALL · IN · A · DAY'S · WORK

ATHLETES

AND

ACTORS

ANITA GANERI

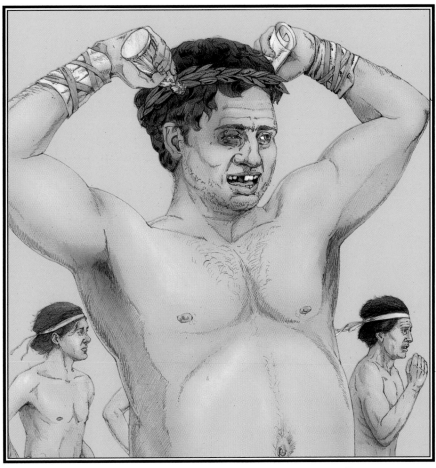

PETER BEDRICK BOOKS
NTC/Contemporary Publishing Group

CONTENTS

Nº 1 • POLITICIAN ┌ι

JOB DESCRIPTION: A TOP JOB FOR THOSE WITH AMBITION. MUST ENJOY A CHALLENGE.
PAY: GREAT WEALTH AND POWER.

Nº 2 • HOPLITE ┌ιιι

JOB DESCRIPTION: RESPECTABLE CAREER SERVING YOUR CITY. PART-TIME OR FULL-TIME AVAILABLE.
PAY: VARIES WITH RANK AND EXPERIENCE.

Nº 3 • SPARTAN Δ

JOB DESCRIPTION: LASTS A LIFETIME. MUST BE OF SPARTAN BIRTH. NOT FOR THE FAINTHEARTED.
PAY: LAND AND SLAVES TO WORK IT.

Nº 4 • ATHLETE Διι

JOB DESCRIPTION: STRENGTH, SKILL, AND STAMINA NEEDED. PREPARE TO TRAIN HARD TO REACH THE TOP.
PAY: HONOR, GLORY, AND SUPERSTARDOM.

Nº 5 • MERCHANT Διιιι

JOB DESCRIPTION: GREAT OPPORTUNITIES FOR ADVENTUROUS TYPES.
PAY: EXCELLENT PROFITS IN EXPANDING BUSINESS.

Nº 6 • TEACHER Δ┌ι

JOB DESCRIPTION: CAREER FOR SMARTY-PANTS ONLY. GOOD COMMUNICATION SKILLS A MUST.
PAY: COMES OUT OF THE SCHOOL FEES.

Nº 7 • SCIENTIST Δ┌ιιι

JOB DESCRIPTION: A CHANCE TO MAKE HISTORY. MUST THINK LOGICALLY.
PAY: GOOD SALARY PLUS PROFITS FROM TEACHING AND FROM WRITING BOOKS.

Nº 8 • DOCTOR ΔΔ

JOB DESCRIPTION: REWARDING CAREER IN UP-AND-COMING PROFESSION.
PAY: VERY GOOD IF YOUR PATIENTS ARE RICH – AND YOU CURE THEM!

Nº 9 • ORACLE ΔΔιι

JOB DESCRIPTION: A RARE OPPORTUNITY FOR GIRLS WITH AN EYE TO THE FUTURE.
PAY: DEPENDS IF PEOPLE LIKE WHAT THEY HEAR.

Nº 10 • ACTOR ΔΔιιιι

JOB DESCRIPTION: YOU TOO CAN BECOME A STAR. TALENT, STAMINA, AND A GOOD MEMORY ESSENTIAL.
PAY: VERY GOOD WHEN YOU'RE TOP OF THE BILL.

Nº 11 • ARCHITECT ΔΔ┌ι

JOB DESCRIPTION: CREATIVE AND HIGHLY SKILLED WORK. MUST BE GOOD AT DRAWING.
PAY: TOP FEES PAID FOR HIGH-QUALITY RESULTS.

Nº 12 • FARMER ΔΔ┌ιιι

JOB DESCRIPTION: SEASONAL WORK – SOWING, PLOWING, WINE-MAKING, AND GOAT-HERDING.
PAY: REASONABLE IF THE HARVEST IS GOOD.

GLOSSARY ΔΔΔ

INDEX ΔΔΔιι

GREEK NUMERALS			
ι 1	Δι 11	ΔΔι 21	ΔΔΔι 31
ιι 2	Διι 12	ΔΔιι 22	ΔΔΔιι 32
ιιι 3	Διιι 13	ΔΔιιι 23	
ιιιι 4	Διιιι 14	ΔΔιιιι 24	H
┌ 5	Δ┌ 15	ΔΔ┌ 25	100
┌ι 6	Δ┌ι 16	ΔΔ┌ι 26	X
┌ιι 7	Δ┌ιι 17	ΔΔ┌ιι 27	1,000
┌ιιι 8	Δ┌ιιι 18	ΔΔ┌ιιι 28	M
┌ιιιι 9	Δ┌ιιιι 19	ΔΔ┌ιιιι 29	10,000
Δ 10	ΔΔ 20	ΔΔΔ 30	

INTRODUCTION

Welcome to Ancient Greece! You've gone back in time almost 2,500 years and arrived in Athens during its "Golden Age." At this time, Greece is divided into lots of city-states, each with its own rulers and laws. Athens is the greatest of these, with Sparta close behind. Take a stroll through the city and see how the people spend their days. A merchant is loading his wares on to his ship in the port. A teacher scolds a lazy pupil. In the theater, the actors are busy rehearsing for tonight's performance.
Will you find the job for you?

IF YOU LIKED PUBLIC SPEAKING and had a thick skin, a career in politics might be for you. In fact, you didn't have a choice. Athens was a democracy. Everyone, rich and poor, had a vote about how the city was run. Well, almost everyone...except women, slaves, foreigners, and people under the age of 18!

Every nine days, you met at the Assembly to debate and pass laws. Anyone could speak but you had to shout loudly to be heard. You might be picked for official duty. Jobs included market inspector, tax collector, and chief of police. If you were lucky, you might end up organizing the Olympic Games.

To vote you out, people wrote your name on a broken bit of pottery. More than 6,000 votes, and it was goodbye to Athens!

JOB DESCRIPTION: A TOP JOB FOR THOSE WITH AMBITION. MUST ENJOY A CHALLENGE.

PAY: GREAT WEALTH AND POWER.

If you were good at your job and had army experience, you might be elected strategos. This was the top job in the government. But woe betide you if you broke any of your promises. You were banished from Athens for ten years if enough people voted against you.

CURRICULUM VITAE
PERICLES

NAME: PERICLES
DATE OF BIRTH: C 495BC
OCCUPATION: ELECTED STRATEGOS EVERY YEAR FROM 443BC-429BC
DISTINGUISHING FEATURES: THE GIFT OF GAB. COULD ALWAYS PERSUADE THE ASSEMBLY HE WAS RIGHT.
SPECIAL ACHIEVEMENTS: BRILLIANT MILITARY LEADER AND POLITICIAN. POPULAR AND POWERFUL. REBUILT ATHENS AFTER THE PERSIANS DESTROYED THE CITY.
DOWNFALL: IN 430BC CHARGED WITH STEALING PUBLIC MONEY AND GIVEN A HUGE FINE. RE-ELECTED BUT DIED IN 429BC DURING THE GREAT PLAGUE OF ATHENS.

At least 6,000 citizens were needed for the Assembly to meet. If numbers were low, the police dragged people in off the streets!

MOST ANCIENT GREEKS preferred to talk problems over. But if their cities were attacked, they were quite ready to fight to save them. Between the ages of 18-20, boys in Athens spent two years training as soldiers. They were then put on a special list and called up if war broke out.

FIGHT A GREEK BATTLE

1. THE HOPLITES FORM A PHALANX, EIGHT ROWS DEEP. YOU HOLD YOUR SHIELD IN FRONT OF YOU, OVERLAPPING WITH YOUR NEIGHBOR'S.

2. YOU MARCH TOWARD THE ENEMY. A FLUTE PLAYER HELPS YOU KEEP IN STEP. YOU SMASH INTO THE ENEMY PHALANX AND PUSH WITH ALL YOUR MIGHT. THE MAN IN FRONT IS KILLED. YOU STEP FORWARD TO TAKE HIS PLACE.

3. AT LAST, THE ENEMY PHALANX GIVES WAY. YOU'VE WON! YOU HANG YOUR WEAPONS IN THE TREES TO THANK THE GODS FOR YOUR VICTORY.

JOB DESCRIPTION: RESPECTABLE CAREER SERVING YOUR CITY. PART-TIME OR FULL-TIME AVAILABLE.

PAY: VARIES WITH RANK AND EXPERIENCE.

You might join the army as a hoplite, or foot soldier. But you had to pay for your own weapons and armor. If you couldn't afford it, you could be a psilos. Then you only had clubs and stones to fight with and an animal skin, not armor.

Two important wars were the Persian Wars between Greece and Persia (490-449BC – Greece won) and the Peloponnesian War between Athens and Sparta (431-404BC – Sparta won).

Athenian hoplites had an "A" on their shields. Spartan hoplites wore red cloaks.

DID YOU KNOW?

The first ever marathon was run in 490BC when an Athenian soldier ran 26.2 miles nonstop from Marathon to Athens. He brought news that the Greeks had beaten the Persians in battle.

WAR REPORT
431BC

WE ARE NOW AT WAR WITH ATHENS. AN INVASION FORCE IS BEING PREPARED. THE KINGS REQUIRE ALL ABLE-BODIED MEN TO REPORT FOR IMMEDIATE DUTY. LONG LIVE SPARTA!

MEET SAMOS. He's a Spartan. This wasn't exactly a career, more something you were born into. But it took a very special sort of person to be a super-Spartan. First of all, you had to be tough. The Spartans wanted to be the greatest city-state in Greece. So they spent their whole lives training for war. They were also scared that their downtrodden slaves (who did all the work) might turn against them.

So the Spartans became the meanest, fiercest soldiers in the world. The worst thing you could call a Spartan was a coward, or "Trembler." This meant he was too scared to fight. You could easily spot a Trembler because of the one-sided moustache he had to grow.

1. YOU LEAVE HOME AT SEVEN YEARS OLD TO LIVE IN AN ARMY BARRACKS. LIFE IS GOING TO BE HARD.

2. YOU JOIN A GROUP OF OTHER BOYS. THE TOUGHEST BOY IS ELECTED LEADER. YOU HAVE A TUNIC TO WEAR BUT NO SHOES.

JOB DESCRIPTION: LASTS A LIFETIME. MUST BE OF SPARTAN BIRTH. NOT FOR THE FAINTHEARTED.

PAY: LAND AND SLAVES TO WORK IT.

Girls didn't fight but they had to keep fit to have healthy babies. They did gymnastics, danced, and ran races. This shocked the rest of Greece!

DID YOU KNOW?

In the barracks, younger boys waited on older boys. If they did something wrong, they were bitten on the back of the hand!

TRAIN AS A SPARTAN

3. YOU SLEEP IN A COLD ROOM ON A BED OF REEDS AND THISTLES.

4. YOU LEARN TO FIGHT AND FOLLOW ORDERS. YOU'LL BE BEATEN IF YOU'RE LAZY OR COMPLAIN.

5. YOU'RE ALWAYS HUNGRY! YOU HAVE TO STEAL FOOD FROM TEMPLES AND FARMS. THIS TEACHES YOU TO BE SNEAKY, A USEFUL SKILL IN BATTLE.

6. WHEN YOU'RE 20 YEARS OLD, YOU JOIN THE ARMY PROPER.

DAILY GREEK
WIN A VIP DAY OUT AT THE OLYMPIC GAMES IN OUR FABULOUS NEW COMPETITION. ALL YOU HAVE TO DO IS COMPOSE AN ODE TO ONE OF THE WINNERS. SEND YOUR ENTRIES TO THE EDITOR (ONLY ONE ODE PER PERSON).

THE OLYMPIC GAMES were held every four years in summer, in honor of Zeus, king of the gods. It was the greatest sporting event in Greece. Athletes came from far and wide, dreaming of Olympic glory. They trained hard for ten months before the Games. Then they, their trainers, and thousands of spectators made their way to Olympia.

On the first day, the athletes went to the Temple of Zeus to swear to abide by the rules. Any athlete caught bribing the judges was sent home in disgrace. Slaves and girls were not allowed to enter. Girls could not even watch. If they did, and got caught, they might be thrown off a cliff.

B ut for lucky winners it was all worthwhile. Prizes included an olive crown cut from the sacred tree, a statue, a victory ode, or poem, and a hero's welcome when you got back home. Not to mention all the fame and fortune! Some athletes might then become professional and have their wages paid by their home cities.

DID YOU KNOW?
Wars were banned for a month during the Olympics so that people could reach the Games safely. This was called the sacred truce. There were heavy fines for breaking it.

YOUR OLYMPIC GUIDE

1. TRACK EVENTS
STADE – 1 LENGTH OF THE TRACK (630 FT)* STAR EVENT*
DIAULOS – 2 LENGTHS OF THE TRACK
DOLICHOS – 24 LENGTHS OF THE TRACK
HOPLITE RACE – CONTESTANTS RUN IN FULL ARMOR

2. PENTATHLON
FIVE EVENTS – RUNNING, WRESTLING, LONG JUMP, JAVELIN AND DISCUS.

3. HORSE RACING
MAIN RACE OF 3/4 MILE.

4. CHARIOT RACING
TWO AND FOUR HORSE RACES. RUN OVER 12 LAPS OF TRACK WITH 40 CHARIOTS IN EACH RACE.

5. IN THE RING
UPRIGHT WRESTLING – THREE THROWS FOR A WIN.
GROUND WRESTLING – UNTIL ONE MAN GIVES IN.
BOXING – AS ABOVE.
PANKRATION – WRESTLING AND BOXING COMBINED.
ANYTHING GOES, EXCEPT BITING, BREAKING FINGERS, OR EYE-GOUGING.

WITH A TASTE FOR ADVENTURE, and an eye for a bargain, why not become a merchant? Every day, merchant ships came and went from the busy port of Piraeus in Athens, loaded with wine, olive oil, and pottery to trade for grain, timber, metals, and slaves.

Merchants also offered lifts to paying passengers.

You might sail to one of the Greek colonies overseas. These had been set up to ease overcrowding and food shortages in Greece. Or you might head for a trading post in Egypt or Sicily.

Wine and oil were carried in large pottery jars, called amphorae. These were packed tightly together in the ship's hold.

Of course, traveling by sea was risky. Ships were rammed by pirates who stole their cargoes, or were wrecked by storms. Dishonest sailors sometimes robbed their passengers. It was wise to make a sacrifice to the sea god, Poseidon, before you set sail. And best not to travel in winter. The safest time to sail was April to September.

If you fancied yourself as a sailor, you could turn up at the port to see if there were any jobs open.

DID YOU KNOW?
In about 325BC, the Greek explorer Pytheas sailed as far as Britain and the Arctic. Sadly, no one back home believed him!

∆r

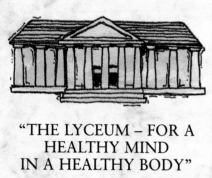

LIMITED PLACES AVAILABLE AT ARISTOTLE'S LYCEUM, ATHENS.

FIRST-CLASS SPORTS' FACILITIES, LECTURE HALLS, AND LIBRARY. FOR AN INTERVIEW, SEE THE ENROLLMENT OFFICER.

"THE LYCEUM – FOR A HEALTHY MIND IN A HEALTHY BODY"

THE ANCIENT GREEKS were very keen on education and being a teacher was a good job to have. There were three types of school. You might run a general school, where you taught the three Rs – reading, writing, and arithmetic. You might run a music school, teaching singing, poetry, and playing the lyre. Or you might run a sports school, training boys to run, wrestle, and use weapons. It depended on what you were good at.

Girls did not go to school. Their mothers taught them at home. Some learned to read and write – most learned spinning, weaving...and housework!

Your pupils were boys from wealthy homes. Poor families couldn't afford the fees. They started school at seven years old, and left at 18 to start their military training.

JOB DESCRIPTION: CAREER FOR SMARTY-PANTS ONLY. GOOD COMMUNICATION SKILLS A MUST.

PAY: COMES OUT OF THE SCHOOL FEES.

THREE TOP THINKERS

SOME OF THE BRAINIEST GREEKS WERE CALLED PHILOSOPHERS. THEY TAUGHT IN SCHOOLS CALLED GYMNASIA. THEY WERE INTERESTED IN QUESTIONS ABOUT THE MEANING OF LIFE.

1. SOCRATES (C 469-399BC)
TAUGHT BY ASKING QUESTIONS ABOUT GOOD AND EVIL. FORCED TO DRINK POISON BECAUSE PEOPLE DIDN'T LIKE HIS NEWFANGLED IDEAS. FAMOUS WORKS: DIDN'T WRITE ANYTHING DOWN.

2. PLATO (C 429-347BC)
PUPIL OF SOCRATES. WROTE ABOUT HOW A CITY-STATE SHOULD BE GOVERNED. FOUNDED THE ACADEMY SCHOOL IN ATHENS. HIS IDEAS ARE STILL STUDIED TODAY. FAMOUS WORKS: THE REPUBLIC.

3. ARISTOTLE (C 384-322BC)
PUPIL OF PLATO. TEACHER OF ALEXANDER THE GREAT. WROTE ABOUT POETRY AND SCIENCE. FOUNDED THE LYCEUM SCHOOL IN ATHENS. FAMOUS WORKS: POETICS, METAPHYSICA.

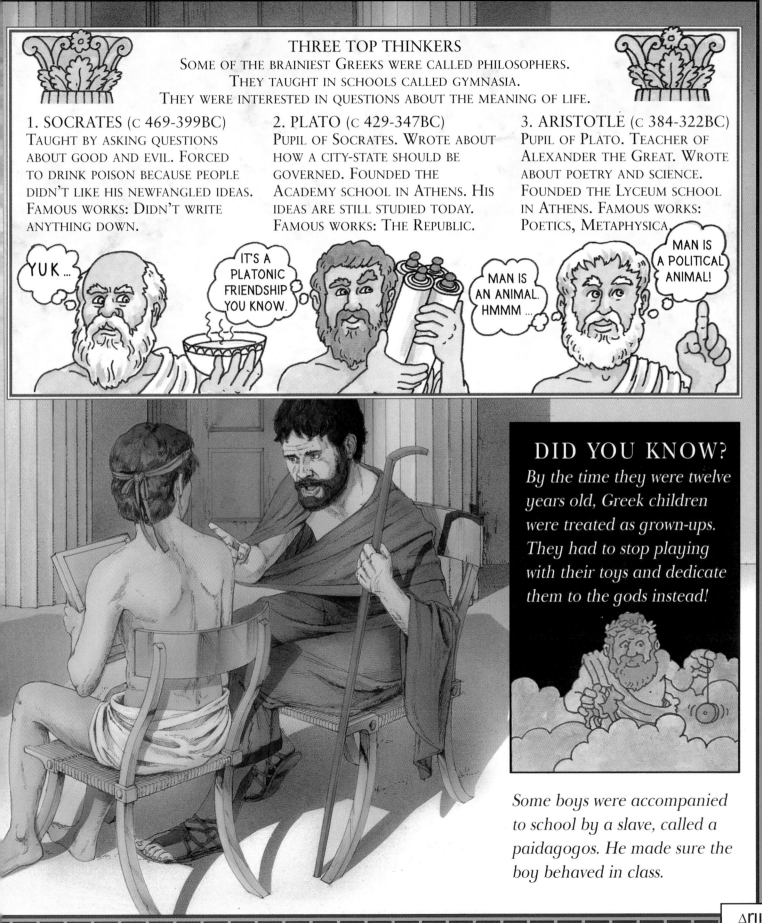

YUK ...

IT'S A PLATONIC FRIENDSHIP YOU KNOW.

MAN IS AN ANIMAL. HMMM ...

MAN IS A POLITICAL ANIMAL!

DID YOU KNOW?

By the time they were twelve years old, Greek children were treated as grown-ups. They had to stop playing with their toys and dedicate them to the gods instead!

Some boys were accompanied to school by a slave, called a paidagogos. He made sure the boy behaved in class.

ASTRONOMER

SEEKS ASSISTANT.
MUST BE HARD-WORKING,
PUNCTUAL, AND WILLING TO
WORK NIGHTS.
INTERVIEWS WILL BE HELD AT
THE NEXT FULL MOON.

CONTACT:
ARISTARCHUS OF SAMOS

DID YOU KNOW?

Legend says that Hypatia of Alexandria, a female mathematician, was so fabulously beautiful that she had to give lectures from behind a screen.

THE ANCIENT GREEKS were brilliant at science, math, astronomy, biology, geography – you name it, they were good at it! Some of their discoveries are still used today. So if you were brainy and curious about the world, a career in science might be for you.

By asking questions and making observations, scientists found new ways of explaining how the world worked. They weren't always popular. Many Greeks still believed that the world was controlled by the gods and saw science as dangerous. On the other hand, students came from far and wide to learn from the great Greek masters.

JOB DESCRIPTION: A CHANCE TO MAKE HISTORY. MUST THINK LOGICALLY.

PAY: GOOD SALARY PLUS PROFITS FROM TEACHING AND FROM WRITING BOOKS.

Anaxagoras explaining that the Moon reflects light from the Sun.

SCIENCE SUPERSTARS

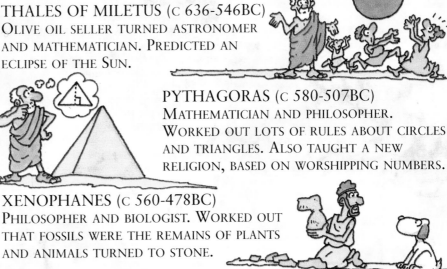

THALES OF MILETUS (C 636-546BC)
OLIVE OIL SELLER TURNED ASTRONOMER AND MATHEMATICIAN. PREDICTED AN ECLIPSE OF THE SUN.

PYTHAGORAS (C 580-507BC)
MATHEMATICIAN AND PHILOSOPHER. WORKED OUT LOTS OF RULES ABOUT CIRCLES AND TRIANGLES. ALSO TAUGHT A NEW RELIGION, BASED ON WORSHIPPING NUMBERS.

XENOPHANES (C 560-478BC)
PHILOSOPHER AND BIOLOGIST. WORKED OUT THAT FOSSILS WERE THE REMAINS OF PLANTS AND ANIMALS TURNED TO STONE.

ANAXAGORAS (C 500-428BC)
ASTRONOMER AND PHILOSOPHER. REALIZED THAT THE MOON REFLECTS LIGHT FROM THE SUN. IT DOESN'T MAKE ANY LIGHT OF ITS OWN.

DEMOCRITUS (C 460-370BC)
PHILOSOPHER AND PHYSICIST. SAID THAT EVERYTHING WAS MADE OF TINY PARTICLES CALLED ATOMS. WHICH IT IS!

ARISTARCHUS (C 310-230BC)
ASTRONOMER. DISCOVERED THAT THE EARTH MOVED ROUND THE SUN. BUT COULDN'T PROVE IT SO NO ONE BELIEVED HIM!

EUCLID (C 300BC)
MATHEMATICIAN. WROTE A BRILLIANT BOOK ON MATH WHICH IS STILL READ TODAY.

ERATOSTHENES (C 275-195BC)
ASTRONOMER AND MATHEMATICIAN. USED MATH TO CALCULATE THE SIZE OF THE EARTH. AND WASN'T FAR WRONG.

ARCHIMEDES (C 287-212BC)
MATHEMATICIAN, INVENTOR, ASTRONOMER. MADE HIS GREATEST DISCOVERY IN THE BATH!

THE DOCTORS' OATH

"I swear by all the gods to carry out this oath.
To respect my teacher like my parents.
To pass on my knowledge to others.
To heal people, not harm them.
Not to give poison to anyone.
Not to carry out illegal operations.
To live a pure and holy life.
And to keep a secret."

THIS OATH was written by Hippocrates, the most famous Greek doctor of all. He founded a medical school on the island of Kos. He made his students swear the oath when they qualified as doctors. Hippocrates taught them to examine patients carefully and look for signs and symptoms of illness. Then they prescribed a cure, often a medicine made of herbs, combined with a good diet and exercise.

Not all Greek doctors were so scientific. Some were priests in the temple of Asclepius, the god of healing. You allowed sick people to spend a night in the temple in the hope that the god would appear in their dreams and show them a cure for their illness. Then you could wait until they woke up – and treat them! What could be simpler?

HIPPOCRATES' TOP TIPS FOR DOCTORS

FOR SETTING AN EXAMPLE TO YOUR PATIENTS

1. KEEP YOURSELF FIT AND HEALTHY.
2. DAB ON A BIT OF PERFUME (NOTHING TOO STRONG).
3. ALWAYS WEAR NEAT, CLEAN CLOTHES.
4. DON'T LOOK TOO HAPPY OR SAD. SOMEWHERE IN BETWEEN IS BEST. (YOU DON'T WANT TO WORRY YOUR PATIENT!)
5. ALWAYS FOLLOW THE HIPPOCRATIC OATH (SEE LEFT).

DO YOU HAVE WHAT IT TAKES?

DID YOU KNOW?

People who were cured by Asclepius left models of the "ill" parts of their bodies to thank the god. These might be ears, eyes, noses, legs, and arms.

Greek doctors used instruments made of iron and bronze. They included forceps and knives. Operations were very painful – the best anesthetic was wine!

GAZE INTO THE
FUTURE
WITH THE GREAT
MADAME CLOTHO
WORLD-FAMOUS MYSTIC AND
SOOTHSAYER

APPEARING IN THE AGORA
ON FRIDAY
BRING YOUR OWN
HOROSCOPE

THE GREEKS WERE VERY SUPERSTITIOUS. They consulted the gods before they did anything, in case the gods disapproved. They also believed the gods could tell the future. So they visited shrines, called oracles, to ask the gods questions and hear their replies. The most famous oracle was at Delphi. Here the god Apollo spoke through his priestess, the Pythia.

To be the Pythia, you had to be born in Delphi. You fasted and bathed in the sacred spring, then took your seat inside the temple, dressed in white. Then you went into a trance and answered people's questions, on Apollo's behalf. The Delphi oracle was so busy that there were two priestesses who took turns to be the Pythia.

JOB DESCRIPTION: A RARE OPPORTUNITY FOR GIRLS WITH AN EYE TO THE FUTURE.

PAY: DEPENDS IF PEOPLE LIKE WHAT THEY HEAR.

MEET THE GREEK GODS

1. ZEUS RULER OF THE GODS AND THE HEAVENS. MASTER OF DISGUISE (BULL, SWAN, SHOWER OF GOLD, ETC). TERRIFYING WHEN ANGRY.

2. HERA GODDESS OF WOMEN AND MARRIAGE. ZEUS'S WIFE. BEAUTIFUL, PROUD, AND HAUGHTY.

3. POSEIDON ZEUS'S BROTHER. GOD OF THE SEA AND OF EARTHQUAKES. LIVED IN AN UNDERWATER PALACE.

4. HESTIA GODDESS OF THE HEARTH AND HOME. GENTLE AND KIND. A SHRINE IN EVERY CITY.

5. PLUTO GOD OF THE DEAD AND RULER OF THE UNDERWORLD. FRIGHTENING AND GLOOMY. VERY RICH.

6. DEMETER GODDESS OF PLANTS AND OF THE HARVEST.

7. APHRODITE GODDESS OF BEAUTY AND LOVE. FICKLE AND VAIN BUT CHARMING.

8. HEPHAESTOS GOD OF CRAFTSMEN AND SMITHS. MADE JEWELRY AND WEAPONS FOR THE OTHER GODS. VERY STRONG.

9. ARES GOD OF WAR. SHORT TEMPERED AND BLOOD-THIRSTY. IN LOVE WITH APHRODITE.

10. ARTEMIS GODDESS OF THE MOON, HUNTING, AND SMALL CHILDREN.

11. APOLLO GOD OF THE SUN, LIGHT, MUSIC, AND TRUTH. TWIN BROTHER OF ARTEMIS.

12. HERMES GOD OF TRAVELERS AND THIEVES. MESSENGER FOR THE GODS.

13. ATHENA GODDESS OF WISDOM, WAR, AND OF ATHENS.

14. DIONYSUS GOD OF WINE AND THEATER. VERY POPULAR.

DID YOU KNOW?

The Corinth Oracle cheated. It claimed you could speak directly to the god. In fact, you were speaking to a priest hidden in a secret passage under the altar!

THE STAGE IS SET, the audience quiet. The play is about to begin ...

The Ancient Greeks loved going to the theater. The most popular plays were tragedies: the gloomier, the better. Open-air theaters sprung up all over Greece. The audience sat in a circle. The best seats were in the front row. These were reserved for important officials and visitors.

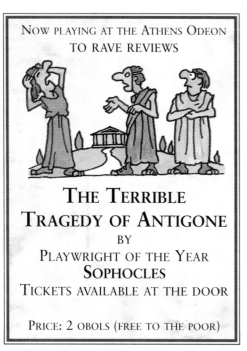

NOW PLAYING AT THE ATHENS ODEON TO RAVE REVIEWS

THE TERRIBLE TRAGEDY OF ANTIGONE
BY
PLAYWRIGHT OF THE YEAR
SOPHOCLES
TICKETS AVAILABLE AT THE DOOR

PRICE: 2 OBOLS (FREE TO THE POOR)

DRESSING THE PART

MASK – YOU WORE DIFFERENT MASKS FOR DIFFERENT CHARACTERS
WIG – IF YOU'RE PLAYING A GIRL
PADDED CLOTHES – TO MAKE YOU EASIER TO SEE
PLATFORM SHOES – TO MAKE YOU TALLER AND EASIER TO SEE
COSTUME – COLORFUL FOR THE HAPPY CHARACTERS, DARK FOR THE TRAGIC ONES

△△
IIII

If you liked dressing up, had a strong voice, and didn't get stage-fright, you might have become an actor. You needed a good memory for learning lines, and lots of energy – some plays lasted all day. And you had to be a man. If you were really good, you might be cast in a starring role. If not, you could still be part of the chorus. A wealthy Greek paid for the play and gave you your wages. Top actors were in demand.

DID YOU KNOW?
One play was so sad, it made the audience cry! Its author was fined 1,000 drachmas for causing so much unhappiness.

STAR FILE

NAME: PHEIDIAS
DATE OF BIRTH: C 500BC
OCCUPATION: SCULPTOR
USEFUL CONTACTS: A CLOSE
FRIEND OF PERICLES
GREATEST ACHIEVEMENTS:
• THE HUGE STATUE OF ATHENA
INSIDE THE PARTHENON. IT WAS
OVER 40 FEET HIGH AND MADE
OF WOOD, COVERED IN GOLD
AND IVORY.
• THE FRIEZE AROUND THE
OUTSIDE OF THE PARTHENON.
• THE GREAT STATUE OF ZEUS AT
OLYMPIA.
DOWNFALL: CHARGED WITH
STEALING MONEY AND GOLD.
DIED IN PRISON IN C 425BC.

BEING AN ARCHITECT was a very good job. The Greeks liked their buildings grand and graceful. You were kept hard at work designing theaters, temples, schools, and public buildings, some of which still stand today. You were paid by the state or by a rich citizen who wanted to make his mark. Many architects started out as masons or carpenters and worked their way up from there.

It helped to have friends in high places. When Pericles ruled Athens (see page rɪɪ), he hired a leading architect, called Ictinus, to design a magnificent temple on the Acropolis hill, dedicated to Athena and called the Parthenon. It took ten years to complete, from 447-438BC. The temple was built of huge slabs of marble, dragged up the hill by ox-cart. They were hauled into place with ropes and pulleys, and fixed with metal pegs. The outside was decorated with colorful painted statues and carvings.

JOB DESCRIPTION: CREATIVE AND HIGHLY SKILLED WORK. MUST BE GOOD AT DRAWING.

PAY: TOP FEES PAID FOR HIGH-QUALITY RESULTS.

PICK A PILLAR

GREEK BUILDINGS WERE FAMOUS FOR THEIR COLUMNS.
THERE WERE THREE STYLES TO CHOOSE FROM:

DORIC – SIMPLE, STURDY COLUMNS WITH PLAIN TOPS. POPULAR ON MAINLAND GREECE.

IONIC – THIN, ELEGANT COLUMNS WITH SCROLL-LIKE TOPS. ALL THE RAGE ON THE GREEK ISLANDS.

CORINTHIAN – MUCH FUSSIER. TOPS DECORATED WITH LEAVES. ONLY CAUGHT ON IN ROMAN TIMES.

EAT LIKE A GREEK

BREAKFAST
BREAD DIPPED IN WINE
MIXED WITH WATER.

FOLLOWED BY
LUNCH
MORE BREAD WITH GOAT'S CHEESE,
OLIVES AND FIGS.

FOLLOWED BY
DINNER
BARLEY PORRIDGE OR BREAD WITH BEANS, AND
VEGETABLES.
MEAT, FISH, AND HONEY CAKES, IF YOU'RE RICH.
AND TO DRINK
WINE MIXED WITH WATER, WATER, AND MILK.

BEING A FARMER wasn't an easy life. The soil was poor and stony, and it didn't rain for months on end. Most farms were small. On them, farmers grew food for their families and a bit extra to sell at market. If the harvest was bad, you could borrow money to help you get by. But if you couldn't pay off your debt, your land was confiscated and you might have to sell yourself and your family into slavery.

Many ordinary Greeks worked as farmers in winter, and sailors in summer.

DID YOU KNOW?
At dinner parties for wealthy Greeks guests wore garlands of laurel leaves on their heads as party hats.

JOB DESCRIPTION: SEASONAL WORK – SOWING, PLOWING, WINE-MAKING, AND GOAT-HERDING.

PAY: REASONABLE IF THE HARVEST IS GOOD.

Other farms were much bigger. They were owned by wealthy Greeks who lived in the city, and were run by bailiffs, or managers. Most of the hardest work was done by slaves.

ON THE FARM
SOME OF THE JOBS YOU MIGHT HAVE TO DO:

1. PLOWING THE FIELDS WITH AN OX-PLOW.

2. SOWING GRAIN – BARLEY AND WHEAT.

3. SHEARING SHEEP.

4. CUTTING GRASS FOR HAY.

5. PRAYING TO THE GODDESS DEMETER FOR A GOOD HARVEST.

6. HARVESTING GRAIN WITH SHARP SICKLES.

7. PICKING AND TREADING GRAPES FOR WINE.

8. KNOCKING OLIVES OFF THE TREES.

9. MAKING GOATS' CHEESE.

10. TENDING THE BEE-HIVES.

GLOSSARY

Acropolis
A hill in Athens on which stood many magnificent temples, including the Parthenon, dedicated to the goddess Athena.

Agora
The open market and meeting place in a city.

Chorus
A group of actors in Greek plays who would speak together, addressing the audience.

Citizen
Men born in Athens who were not slaves. All citizens, rich or poor, were allowed to vote.

City-state
A city and the countryside around it. Ancient Greece was divided into lots of city-states.

Colony
One of many places abroad where Greeks went to live when Greece itself got too overcrowded.

Democracy
A system in which everyone has a say about how their country, or city, is governed.

Drachma
A silver coin used in Athens. It is still used as Greek currency today.

Hippocrates
A famous Greek doctor who taught in a medical school on the island of Kos. Doctors still follow his ideas today.

Hoplite
A foot soldier in the army. He wore heavy armor. In battle, hoplites fought in a block of soldiers eight rows deep.

Kings
Sparta had two royal families and two kings who ruled together. Their main responsibility was to lead their armies in battle. In peacetime their duties were only as religious leaders.

Oracle

A sacred place where people went to consult a god. They asked the god questions. Then a priest or priestess answered them on behalf of the god.

Pericles

Strategos of Athens from 443-429BC. A brilliant general and a very powerful and popular leader.

Philosopher

A very clever Greek teacher who studied politics, human behavior and science. Philosophers asked questions about how the world worked.

Sophocles

A famous Greek playwright. He wrote over 100 plays, although only seven still survive. He won many first prizes at the Athens Drama Festival.

Strategos

A powerful general. In Athens, ten generals were elected every year.

Trireme

A Greek warship with three rows of oars.

INDEX

A

Acropolis 26, 30
actor 24, 25, 30
Alexander the Great 17
Anaxagoras 19
Aphrodite 23
Apollo 22, 23
Archimedes 19
architect 26
Ares 23
Aristarchus 19
Aristotle 16, 17
army 10, 11
Artemis 23
Asclepius 20, 21
Assembly 6, 7
astronomer 19
Athena 23, 26
athlete 12, 13
author 25

B

bailiffs 29
biologist 19

C

carpenters 26
chorus 25, 30

D

Delphi 22
Demeter 23, 29
Democritus 19

Dionysus 23
doctor 20, 21
Draco 7

E

Eratosthenes 19
Euclid 19
explorer 15

F

farmer 28, 29

H

Hephaestos 23
Hera 23
Hermes 23
Hestia 23
Hippocrates 20, 21, 30
hoplite 8, 9, 13, 30
Hypatia 18

I

Ictinus 26
inventor 19

J

judges 12

K

kings 10, 30
Kos 20

M

Marathon 9
market inspector 6
masons 26
mathematician 18, 19
merchant 14

O

oarsmen 8
Olympic Games 6, 12, 13
oracle 22, 23

P

paidagogos 17
Parthenon 26
Pericles 7, 26, 31
Pheidias 26
philosophers 16, 17, 19, 31
physicist 19
Piraeus 8, 14
pirates 15
Plato 17
Pluto 23
police 6, 7
politician 6, 7
Poseidon 15, 23
priestess 22
priests 20, 23
psilos 9
Pythagoras 19
Pytheas 15
Pythia 22

S

sailor 15, 28
scientist 18
slaves 10, 12, 29
Socrates 17
soldiers 8, 9, 10
Sophocles 24, 31
Spartan 9, 10, 11
strategos 7, 31

T

tax collector 6
teacher 16
Thales of Miletus 19
Trembler 10

X

Xenophanes 19

Z

Zeus 12, 23, 26

GREEK NUMERALS			
I	1	ΔΓII	17
II	2	ΔΓIII	18
III	3	ΔΓIIII	19
IIII	4	ΔΔ	20
Γ	5	ΔΔI	21
ΓI	6	ΔΔII	22
ΓII	7	ΔΔIII	23
ΓIII	8	ΔΔIIII	24
ΓIIII	9	ΔΔΓ	25
Δ	10	ΔΔΓI	26
ΔI	11	ΔΔΓII	27
ΔII	12	ΔΔΓIII	28
ΔIII	13	ΔΔΓIIII	29
ΔIIII	14	ΔΔΔ	30
ΔΓ	15	ΔΔΔI	31
ΔΓI	16	ΔΔΔII	32